I0581214

father forgive me

DESHAWN MCKINNEY

Published by Black Sunflowers Poetry Press
www.blacksunflowerspoetry.com

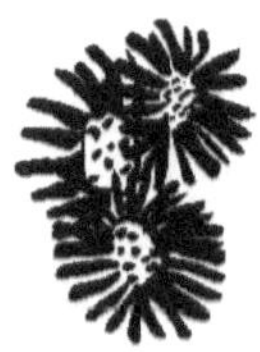

ISBN: 978-1-8382516-4-2

TABLE OF CONTENTS

INTRO NOTE

Black Sunflowers called out and from across the globe, poets answered. The cries of being and feeling were strange, funny, primal, otherworldly, and angry. Poems raged and fluttered, moaned, and muttered, soared and stumbled. From all the speakings, this voice was heard.

Enjoy,

Geffen Bankir
Amanda Holiday

On water

it is late summer, the leaves slow bleed
into the razor winds of fall and I am dreaming
of water — Lake Michigan, the Thames, and other bodies
I know only as backdrops in films —
in my sleep they are protagonists
antiheroes who kill only by the negligence
of those they nourish: there is no malice,
and this is no comfort. I find myself
watching waves swallow cities hole before bed
having felt the belly of a similar beast
but this one would snow if it was sky
and in that I feel home

I am writing this prayer, that sounds like suicide
but reads as a love poem, and it is
both, enough to drink and drown.

Black Hawk Down

my favorite movie is a memory of who you might have been;

there was a time of tenderness
of breath-taking hugs, mountaintop views
of Milwaukee atop your shoulders,
love with an open chest, of marveling at blood
pulsing in harmony

my blood in blood stripes, a sight in dress blues,
being a Marine felt like the only destiny
worth living for, and you lived for me, worked
for me by helping others heal, taking temps and setting bones
in new fatigues, the scrubs of a citizen soldier

I am told these memories were real once
but like all ancient history, we'd be remiss to believe
without evidence and you know how it is,
like the line about when the first bullet zips past?
never talked much about your service but to guess,
you were a marksmen?

Semper fidelis

never spoke on your service so I bought every book on the Marine Corps,
learned Chesty Puller, Carlos Hathcock, every battle rifle and creed;

when I weighed myself and tipped 200 you called me bubble butt
I stepped off, asked my brother if he could teach me how to do a push up.

never explained why you'd go shopping and only come back with beer,
learned to not let you "borrow" money, memorized the best hiding spots

when I had my first kiss, I didn't think anyone would believe me,
had questions about sex but settled for proving you wrong about sexuality

you never taught me how hands could have value beyond threat,
learned to tie ties rewinding Youtube clips in the bathroom before events;

when I lost my virginity Yeezus spun softly in the background,
knew then sex was corrupted, a rebellion against who you broke me into;

you never when I you never when I you never when I you never when I you
never when I you never when I you never when I you never when I

you never explained why you hate me so I have been filling in the blanks
I think it was always about you, I think there must be some way forward

knowing that.

Treatise on love

I have never seen you hit anyone
with your fists, which has taught me
there are many ways to break
things you love:

I learned that voiceless translates to stripped of
speech, gutted and spoken of, spoken for,
mangled throats easily spot a firm grip
some skills are more useful than others
for finding lost things, some things are not
lost is no euphemism for taken

I learned you break them young,
and often, but only have to bite them once
for every bark to become enough

I have never seen you hit anyone
perhaps that is why I missed the signs,

watched Black Hawks fireball
into Somali streets strewn with dust and shell casings,
knees held tight to chest on your bedroom floor;
watched Obama swagger up to a podium on CP time
and stumble over his words through the announcement:
we got bin Laden; watched the yellow tape
erected around some body, somebody's baby
shot in the sun around the corner;

watched us watch these bodies and failed to realize
it was the easiest way for you not to see
yourself, that being close does not mean
coming together and that distinction, too, is how
to break a thing.

Home

Is where I must flee to feel
most myself, it is a marble block
from which to chip necessities

back all heavy with bootleg dvds
boarded windows and gated doors
crumpled fenders, obscene exhausts
lip smackin mothers who laugh like thunder
and grannies who yell when you bring outside scents in;
big booties in sundresses and the eyes glued on them
glasses with anti glare coating so I can look
directly at the diamonds dancin in the UPS driver's mouth
pockets runneth over with city bus rappers, knowing glances
exchanged, careful peeks after the pop of firecrackers
when ain't no independence to be celebrated;
heads ringin with the motorcades of speeding sirens
and memories of a world seen through window panes
within which I became intimate with the process of unmaking—
the sharp crack of faggot and fat and ass fired
at my chest, the impossible length of a duplex hallway
when a barking dog sits at the other end,
how easy you trip when that dog doesn't heel
after being reminded its name is Father, the pressure
at which self-esteem is penetrated by canines
the incessant dig and wondering how long it must take
to retrieve what is buried—

home is where I must flee
to do my best work
soon I will have carved a full face.

You look just like your father / With the homies

I
I am as close to swimming
as I've ever been when this bottle
tips empty, my father's son

> Saturday nights are for the homies,
> yes we'll earn our degrees and settle into our jobs
> but for at least this night it's fuck all that other shit,
> so I am at Morrison's weighing what to mix
> into this Jameson while I text my niggas the addy;

III
my first sip of beer came unceremoniously,
a trip to the liquor store and back, an offer
like a DNA test, next the smell and swallow;
did I know then that it was strong enough
to dissolve a man?

> something about Saturday nights
> makes remembering work, and tonight
> the only work that matters is sung 72 times
> by Rihanna from trunk rattle speakers in my flat,
> and tomorrow my neighbors will leave
> a note as if me and the homies won't run that back
> next weekend.
>   I mix whiskey and ginger beer
> between shots of tequila, rotate my hips into a sweat
> and Shaku Shaku my ass out the door at midnight
> we loud, happy, we free those six blocks to Mojo's
> float from ID check to center of dance floor
> in 3 seconds flat and crown ourselves king,
> or queen,

or some bodies
words do an injustice to because in that moment, then
and there we are, simply, we are.

V
sober through all of high school
and undergrad, no mixing the mixers I red cupped juice
listened to strangers slur their way through praise
like I wish I could do that, responded I just don't feel the need
when what I meant was I have seen a man rot
and my last name is a ledge I can't yet walk safely

leave when the DJ doubles down on songs
we don't like, talk to strangers in English
and Spanish and Swahili on our way to another bar
whose dance floor is smaller
we remain just as big, and free and present until 3am
sleepy cab rides and warm beds or sweat licked off
chests sucked tongues suck everywhere sex
because maybe something happens
before next Saturday

VII
Saturday nights are for the homies and I
wish some things were sacred but even this embracing
the liquid in your hips is about power, about how
attitude and alcohol mix well when you have been practicing
how to survive your whole life; and even that is about something,
like how your father woozied himself in beer cans
and you being so afraid of becoming zombie
that you'd be sober still if all alcohol came in a can.

REM

I kill my father every night
when I close my eyes
and for that I am jealous;

of the two of us,
he gets to sleep.

Scorched earth

recall the first joy
of a bare passport, wonder
of a foreign visa

        remember remember the Chinese restaurant
        Chinatown, fingers sewn together too soon
        you say I move slow. we're young enough to die
        slow I think

next time, you kiss me, something less than
French but enough tongue to be
the English Channel

        the cafe, each poem in competition
        with the buzz of coffee sputtering into cups
        we rode the tube in heat. we're old enough to die,
        now I think

your room was cozy, dim Christmas lights
slung across polaroids of people I'll never meet
I imagine they would have liked me, if we ever met

        the morning after and I am hugging a stranger
        already, wonder if you know I'll never see this room
        a second time, wonder if I am capable of seconds
     I think
        men like me are shirts lifted/thrown, lost somewhere
        until morning, a ritual: shirt pants rings—scattered,
        collected—afraid we're the beasts who raised us,
        or the failures they claimed us, but tempted the same

Memento mori freestyle

tat on my chest a memento mori / grew up and learned to reclaim my
story / angels wit me yellin "you the one!" / Devil on me, "you ya
father's son" / whiskey tippin til the bottle is empty / Lord as my
shepherd I'm through with the envy / pity me not, though I know I'm a
bastard / 3rd degree, this my second master

skin shed myself to a boisterous Black
all stretchmarked arms and heart for this soft,
hugging free the boy once gnawed on and scoffed
at, don't they know roses grow in those cracks?
ain't somebody told them niggas relax?
shackles are made hard, some prison is bought
into, why die ourselves spectre, back lost?
who can kill us but us? come steal this Black?

theft poses a rhetorical question,
I am we is a walking history
survived on the sorcery of lessons
taught across time and oceans, wishfully;
I, emerging from corn bread and blessings;
I, inevitable, and blistering

I don't want exposure, just pay me my money / if you ain't got it, let's
keep it a hunnid / fuck a diamond, I'm the nigga dancin / hoppin flights
like I'm Richard Branson / tat on my chest a memento mori / grew up
and learned to reclaim my story / angels wit me yellin "you the one!" /
Devil on me, "you ya father's son"

northside northside run it

Don't send me flowers

                        when I'm dead
don't send me flowers when I'm not,
while I'm here, I don't like flowers all that much
though I respect them so we can be neighbors
send flowers to my neighbors

in my name

let me pretend I know how to be one
a flower that is, like a neighbor is or a neighbor
like a flower is, let me pretend I am as vivid
though I am not, am black in skin and nature
though not by nature — this is the lack of
nurture you have heard about,
                                        I am.

REM II

tonight I save you,
and it is just
as jarring as dragging the blade
across your belly; I haven't slept
for months and I am reminded
of a time when we went places together,
I remember a time, you missing a stair and falling,
how I didn't laugh and I didn't feel
vindicated, but I did feel pain in my chest
like you must have in your back and I came to you,
helped you, to stand again.

Snapshots of a nigga, in search of

Paris. a new year, lit Arc guiding the flood. a man, learning to boy;
a freedom tower, not unlike a Louvre, far too similar
to empire. destiny manifests but knows only Western genius
is a boosters' myth. you need not get close, her eyes follow
you everywhere, like a regret;
      if eyes are windows, she's a snitch

     Hol' up wait

in Cambridge, folks dress like they attend Hogwarts, & snitch
like the boys got to be men who got to be boy
    without regret,
          got to be similar,
like they make the rules, & rules are meant to be followed
like freedom is the only magic & rules made in its stead are genius.

     I'mma buy my mom a home in Stockholm I'm never home / I'm
     making home wherever homies congregate that's all I know /
     I'm on the road

to bury Babel in Kingston's sugar cane, genius
here, I am light enough to be a snitch;
a team of hair triggers watches through iron sights, barrels follow
& I'm home—metal detectors beep in rimshot, the music of boy-
hood; there, the shiver of snowflakes & searing of flesh are similar
when every body is a full moon, waiting to become a regret

     to Babylon / see Farrakhan at Temple 7, / hashish smoke
     blowin out the roof of 911s / coupe the proof that we in Heaven
     / peace to Proof cuz he in Heaven / brother born on 9-11, older
     than Biggie was / we gon die like Biggie does,

this third time in Heathrow I hide my face; an affair with regret.

I play big bank take little bank with LSE, who thinks itself genius,
& I remember the disposition of all fools is similar.
a roof leaks & I think it's the Russians, still I don't snitch;
when I'm assured it's the snow, I apologize to the boy
in me for ruining his spy moment. perhaps another will follow

> *keep the faith / in God above, keep that .50 in da club / no*
> *more slaughter in the streets / home is hardly home when*
> *homies losin cabbage over beef / last week, my bro called me*
> *said his homie bit a bullet / asked me if the ACA would cover*
> *costs if momma couldn't / momma couldn't*

Tokyo. every morning we run for the train, no one follows
me around, so I steal for the first time, taking joy with no regret.
swimming in Shibuya Crossing I find the only other Black boy;
the mirror in his mouth keeps us alive, I'm struck by his genius
he nods & I promise not to snitch
I visit Fujisan & promise something similar

> *hol' up*

Norwich. a group of poets fear dating they who are similar,
I drink it up and still feel thirsty. maybe I shouldn't follow
unspoken rules? the wine touches my hair and I finally snitch,
leave the housewarming a parliament of hips, full of regret,
the happy kind which whispers that I'm a genius,
the happy kind sacrificed too young in every Black boy

> *hol' up   hol' up*
> *wait*

Milwaukee, similar to my first regret,
trapped in turf war between snitch and genius
the eyes are barrels that follow the poles, and split the boy.

It comes in twos

don't worry about biting off more
choke saying I love you
(it tastes better)

there are only two kinds
the one that smothers
your oxygen & the one that leaves you
to drown

i learned this at Wisconsin Dells
down a slide down into
pride before i knew ego by name;
my words waterlog on sunny days still

i am afraid of drowning
and like all thinking men
i am enamored with water

i learned how to man like oil spill
that sudden, swallowing the muck
wanting to believe some harms are accidents
knowing some accidents are

like all thinking men two disappoints me
and i believe there is another way
like all thinking men i will drown
bitter and smiling, knowing i chose the only path.

Stretchmarks

follow the lines and find yourself
before men named you fat ass and pussy
before men made you stand on scales
before men learned about roses and concrete,
taught you how flowers wilt and bruised your soul
into cement

follow the lines as you were meant to,
rigorously, as you have fled their guidance
before men made you believe in perfect
before you realized the trick, that under the bark
they were lost too, hurt too, worshipping false gods
for fear of reconciling their interiors with their masks

follow them back to before
man up where you were forced to leave
the boy, him fat fingered and sensitive
find him,
tell him that vulnerability is a muscle
squeeze his cheeks
tell him that his brain is enough,
that he is enough
remind him

make sure, if nothing else, he knows this:
he is loved.

Untitled

You pissed on our bedroom carpet like of course this is what happens after they know your name at the liquor store & we turned it into another elephant like why do you take me to the liquor store with you like the five dollars you stole the five dollars that felt like five hundred back then while I pretended to sleep eyelids shut tight like maybe I won't have to open them anymore so I put a lock on my weights so you couldn't use them & I smashed your cds & you called me a faggot maybe not for that but enough times to forget my name anyway & anyway I gave you bus fare to get to the job interview at K Mart but only for one way knowing I couldn't trust you & you wore a suit that olive green suit you wear in the pictures on the wall & I paused the movie when you got home so I could hear how it went because Thermopylae happened and the past can wait but this was happening & I felt guilty because you were trying & that was fifteen years ago and it's a Target now & you visit but as a customer because you haven't worked since & last time we shared space you threatened to snap my neck & next time we share space I hope you reach for me because I left my patience in England by which I only mean I am exhausted & some burdens collapse the spine when carried across borders & I was told to stand up straight though not by you just something I heard around learned around how I learned to live to be to love & I am alive still alive still

Two questions for another life

1.
If you ever come up for air, if ever
the cans run dry and you walk to the Veterans Affairs Center,
or turn left towards Pick n Save instead of the local liquor store, if
you apply for a job again, and if you hear back
and make it to the job interview, if you are hired
and survive the first day and the second and then months
pass, then a year, if you (re)learn how to read mirrors
and remember the language of self reflection, if
you apologize to your mother for calling her a bitch,
for losing her house, for losing her son, if you apologize
to yourself for going Devil Dog and leaving the dog behind,
for forgetting where you left him or refusing to search,
if that day ever comes when you surface for air,
will you be able to forgive that man?

2.
And if you do none of these things, if instead
you turn right on the block and continue
to line your stomach in beer, if you continue to lie,
telling the neighbors you work the night shift
if you must claim theatre as your profession
and pretend as your most valued possession,
if you aim to make good on your word,
reach to snap my neck like you once did
my spirit, if you make me hurt you,
will I be able to forgive you?

for you have sinned

In my earliest memory I am five,
there is a sidewalk on which I am running, maybe
marveling at how the sky got all the way up
there, wanting to ask if God was a painter,
maybe in those seconds it felt possible to learn how to control
a brush, maybe I thought about asking for one I don't know
or won't remember because I am five, there,
legs out and not yet too chubby to be fed affection, on a sidewalk
under a clear sky and my feet catch in the cracks,
God's canvas disappears and I see red everything is red I am
red, cement chews through my knee, someone's hands carry me
somewhere that looks like home and I am red tears hot,
burning face and scalding knee and somewhere close you are
a drill sergeant, familiar, without hesitation, like you've been here
before: stop crying, man up! a Marine again, like you've been
shot 3 times so your son should
dismiss this pain, and this is profound;

I know that is what a man is, even how
to become one. but a boy?

On forgiveness

somewhere you read forgiveness
& dream about killing a man

you hear forgiveness unburdens & check
that the knife is still by your pillow, sometimes
you feel sorry & remember your father's words, how you suck
in your stomach in mirrorless rooms & take pride
in no one believing you were ever that big, in your resurrection;
you tell yourself that you are a man
now, but every night write a hymn for the boy
who tried to scrub his stretch marks into oblivion
you think of what he would have been
if worshipped, if celebrated instead of sacrificed
wonder what to set upon an altar for sensitive Black boys,
regret the threat of the knife but polish the metal, re-set it anyway,
having learned young that sensitive Black boys were fighters
of the world's accord, learned young that you would have to
unlearn your tears but learned how to store them for one day;
you remind yourself that it's never too late to get an education,
hope one day is less tomorrows away when you awake;
next to the blade will be a letter addressed to Black women,
handwritten, for fixing you plates of collard greens & pig's feet
as large as the table, calling you baby & weighing your report cards
heavier than the digits on any bathroom (hallwaylivingroom) scale;
you tell yourself you are a man now, that you say I love you
to the homies without context & hope it sounds as soft as you
believe love needs to be; on the most tender nights you scroll
through memories of smiles hugs travels & sex to pre-empt
the dreams.

you wake to the stillness of 4am, having read about forgiveness,
somewhere, & forgive yourself for having trouble finding it.

Boy Speaks to the River Jordan

I'm a mess momma, stressed
momma, full belly and out east
now, hair down and carefree but blue, blessed
Black and guilty as ever for this peace   ,
and quiet, I only got the whispers
gonetoosoons with stolen vocals for stanzas—
only the ones not bout the dead— figures,
they more heartbeat than me when my hands up
I'm more free, my struggle calloused hands cough
dust on infinity's fingers, remnants
         the oncechild I disappeared; what I wrought
         reaped on 68th, eviction: penance.
                        I, have jumped off the cliff wit all of my
                              I, have landed in the sky wit all my

                              I, landed in the sky wit all of my
            and momma, we safe. these streetlights pray[er]
               powered. I am learning how to say my
                              name in holy letters, the sonics flare
                                 memory: 3 brothers, 68th St
                        grass (we have grass!), garden dirt, cry
                        in mirror, Eve stares back over the sink
                        how to be enough? when you had to tri-
                        mester a fourth time for your trinity.
                        boy as man/mishap in the same period
                  accident sentenced to run-on divinity?
                  i flee tears from our garden, cast stones to a pyramid
         Eve watches, sees a sister in my place
         afro like snake: resting Medusa face

her afro like   resting Medusa face
instead, man body, apple like Adam
stretchmarks just like you momma, but spit mace
like father, son carries his nameburden as atom
funeral, never seen man but die   (quick)

many ways to die a man: slang rock, sang rock rock
pockets, pop rocks in mouth/talk slick 'til the chemicals mix
ever meet a real man momma?   (pro'ly not).
if girls are sugarspiceandeverythingnice of course
we prayed the doctor give us Type 2 on the playground
boys are predictable or, real? Remorse
ourselves back to innocence, a safe sound
the men we had been before we been loud
the men we have lost and now we have found.

the men we lost and found, very profound
        thinkin of me momma, huh? yes I'm blessed
        momma, you stressed, still home, complain no sound
            'cept yo thin blood lip smackin winterstress
            I'll work you eternal summer someday
                supernova your justprayonit, devout
            wide mouthed, laughter licked flesh (someday)
                fish and spaghetti plates, hot sauce, without
        the church, (at breakfast) why we stop goin to church?
                (at dinner) when do God visit the poor?
                checkin my pillow every 15th and first
            here sometimes feels safe though, after the war:
                the angels come cut losses every time,
            some momma drowned 'in her gonetoosoon's pride

I once saw a momma drown   as she cried
            God (They sent messengers wit yellow tape
to package a new angel); ain't you say we all angels who tried?
whose razor backbones once were wings, Bible thick at the nape,
    that I once flew to Medina and back on a school night?
that we once wade in water in all white, came out that nectar
        popsicle sticky yet all Black and alright
            will we be all-right? I tried to Mecca
            for me and myself but I see I need
            help, even the flyest angels need wind
            momma. even Jesus and his Black need
            help, his skin loud, even over our sins;

I know you see me/myself walk his shoes
learning (trying) to carry my name bulletproof

my name carry (clip) my wings bulletproof
I am sprout from your roots but my name ain't
baptised in you? I don't know how to find truth
in that absence, maybe maybe i can't
carrying a father like liquor store
after the Marines, name like KIA
in my best cursive; it taught me to hoard
love to protect love when the dress blues fade
learned best from seeing granny's palms stronghold
everything, watching her full hands lurch
empty how all towers dread to go cold:
with a loud crash and the ending[less] search
for survivors you don't truly believe;
but then digging is how some of us grieve

digging then to hollow out all this grief
—forgive me for the sins of my father—
to question me answered, momma, at least
do you ever dig? am I a bother
if I ask how dirt deep go your shovel?
and do shovels sometimes come in nonstick
cuz maybe I want this to be subtle
and does a child sometimes come in lovesick,
how daughter can come as a son sometimes?
like how I came third after she didn't
like all the men I know   the crime
is the men I know   I am the men I know   hidden
from ourselves our selves self prison, miss bail
and steel   every thing   must go, well

everything must go well and I'll be
home soon, these pockets all full of degrees

empty of myself hoping you stuff me
whole. give me cornbread sweet as skittles please
kiss my Black hair music hoodies safe, call
me boy how you call me when you forget
my name, it lights the way home; hug me small
in your lap like I'm your never-regret
        and the world can't tell you nothin no mo'
        bout your baby, I'm too tall to see you
        in your eyes but none of me can outgrow
        the roots you smiled into my spine. I knew
you would always be close enough to breeze
me calm; I hear your hymns shaking the trees

        momma, your hymns shake every tree but still
            the fruits of your labor somehow seedless
            and you never do whine, you stay so trill
            thuggin your way through each/every season
                thug it out wit me momma, the trauma
                dug a cavity into our namesake[s]
                let me write you a canary momma
                let me write a better chapter than fate
            let me thug it out for you, you just rest
        now momma, go sleep a summer slumber
        when it's cold in, let me warm you a crest
        how the city don't won't ain't no wonder
        you been trill, you been thug, you been angel
        now be warm, be free now, you been faithful

            so faithful to this polar existence,
        I been lost and I been foundin my own
        knees in the dirt, dirt on my knees, missin
            you by the width of a Bible unknown
            to me— yet I am— are angels careful
        wit their wings momma? truth told, is this God
        wrathful if we aren't or don't know where to
            fly or crumble? They listenin, just nod
                or blink or fly if the answer is yes

and momma, I bet you can fly real good.
like a high note if I had to guess,
or or any body from any hood
gonetoosoon; I see you in my eyes you
flight better than you don't, better you do

better that you do flight
momma, do it how you do laughter
do math, flip a funny bone to the right
angle and your Black wings soar like pastor
preacher, saving a wretch like me, like you
could save yourself from the yourself man made
when he put his hands   and there a Death grew
inside me; all those hands, hours delayed,
gracing your wings, I know you fly, ghetto
girls always catch the wind when they go strut
you a lip smackin loud laughin ghetto
angel of a woman, catch wind you must
not catch yourself this time, just fall skyward
kiss the hoodies safe there then fall higher

I can't wait for you to kiss my hoodies safe
(no weapon ever formed against me shall
prosper) pray for me proper, pray my face
out of the news momma, to a new now
that braids my hair like that can't don't won't ain't
enough to get me gonestoosoon walkin
home (cuz I can't won't ain't never no saint
no saint get they hair braided or talkin
like they get they hair between legs braided
or walk like they talk like they get they hair
braided) pray for me? pray me back sacred
put holy on my name when I'm not there
I, want to be, 'fore the streetlights come on
on my way back back to Milwaukee, home

I'm, on my way now momma, back back Home
where the block hottest when the streets frigid
hearted, homies dance basements to warzone
homies be homies even when trippin
am I trippin to think these scholarships
ain't as sweet as red kool-aid and skittles?
the receptions still make my backbones itch:
all the wine, my nameburden the vittles
it's Irish? he asks. pro'ly, I cough slaves
sometimes, dusty remnants of the onceblood
y'all disappeared. no more wine please, behave
sometimes, ask questions to your god above.
honest momma, just watch the sky closely
I am become Daughter, Son, holyhol-
&
I'm a mess Momma, stressed Momma, blessed
Momma, landed in the sky wit all my belief—
men we had lost and now we have found (less
of)— wings diggin in my back like I'm a form of grief,
like everything is & every thing must,
    but my name carry well like bulletproof
    like how your hymns shake trees to holy bloom
      and you braid my curls to snake, like Medus'
      like a woman drowned in her gonetoosoon
      but you fly better than you don't, so do
        be warm now, be free now, you been trill
    please kiss my hoodies an angel backbone,
I'm on my way now momma, back back Home.

To the Homies

Special shout out to the team at Black Sunflowers Poetry Press for taking on this manuscript and giving it a home, for taking this leap with me and the other poets. I'm grateful to have my first book drop as part of their vision.

To Brotha Man, for showing me what a man could and should be, for being the one who always loved me for who I was

To Nika, for reminding me that I had tender spots, believing in my dreams and my ability to reality them

Love.

Black Sunflowers Poetry Press

Backed by an array of artists, activists, poets and poetry fans from all walks of life Black Sunflowers, the UK's first crowdfunded poetry press, came into being in March 2020 with a pledge to publish and promote the work of women, older women and black poets from the UK and around the world. Black Sunflowers is grateful to Nat West's #BackHerBusiness scheme, all the supporters including Patrick Bill, Amanda Sebestyen, Cathy Greenhalgh, Rehana Zaman, Rob Curry, Nadine Marsh-Edwards, Rosa Fong, Judah Attille, Elinor Perry-Smith, Monika Baker, David Curtis, Oona Hyland, Janice Cheddie, Simone Alexander, Mustapha Feika, Michael Cadette and others who wish to remain anonymous, as well as the additional enterprise finance awarded to us. Black Sunflowers is thankful to those who have offered encouragement and advice along the way and who have contributed their skills or inspired through their own publishing entrepreneurship.

Embarking on this venture during Covid19, on the cusp of a lockdown was challenging and perhaps folly. Yet, with daily life on hold, this has been a time for deep reflection for all of us. A time perhaps to pause for poetry.

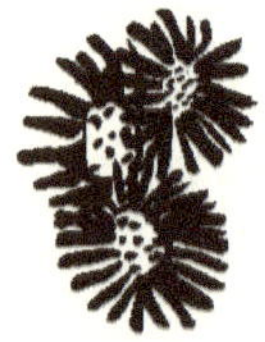

9 781838 251642